ZEST
IS
BEST!

POEMS

by HARVEY
JACKINS

To meet the test,
Free the oppressed
Can still be pressed
Although distressed;

But hurt confessed,
Discharge expressed,
The mind's at rest.
We act with zest.

TABLE OF CONTENTS

A LONG TIME AGO

"THE MEANINGFUL HOLIDAY"

GLOOM AND DOOM

DOGGEREL

SONG LYRICS

UNCLASSIFIED

FOREWORD

One of the fringe benefits of the rediscovery and development of the discharge and recovery process which we call Re-evaluation Counseling has been the emergence of a large number of poets among the co-counselors in the R.C. Communities. It seems plain, after twenty some years, that every human being, underneath any obscuring patterns, is a poet, who takes delight in using language well for elegant communication. Hundreds of co-counselors have written poems and shared them with me, or read them at workshops, or had them published in Present Time (the Re-evaluation Counseling newsletter).

This universal interest in poetry, flourishing in every individual once the emotional blocks are out of the way, has encouraged me to place this collection of poems in print.

Some of the poems were written before my participation in Re-evaluation Counseling. A few are expressions of the distresses from which R.C. has been helping to free me. The great bulk of the poems are intimately tied up with the exciting development of R.C. and the growing and flourishing communities of loving, aware, supportive, and mutually appreciative people who call themselves Co-counselors.

PREFACES were poems written to introduce various pamphlets and books written by me or by others about Re-evaluation Counseling.

POEMS OF COUNSELING are poems I was moved to write by excitements I felt about the counseling process or particular co-counselors.

A LONG TIME AGO harks back to my troubled,
but interesting, youth.

THE MEANINGFUL HOLIDAY is a series of
communication poems sent to other co-counselors
at Christmas and New Years by our original group
at Personal Counselors.

GLOOM AND DOOM is a familiar theme in much
other poetry, but one quite uncommon in my own.
The poems attempt a clear expression of the
emotional content of a distress pattern. To put them
on paper was to separate them somewhat from me,
and was therefore useful.

DOGGEREL includes poems I wrote for a
purpose, that is, to sum up a workshop or similar
"jobs" where the communication required was not
of the loftiest kind.

SONG LYRICS are attempts on my part to
communicate well through that elegant communica-
tion form, the song. Many of these pre-date
Re-evaluation Counseling or are concerned with
other themes.

UNCLASSIFIED is just that.

ZEST IS BEST is respectfully dedicated to all
poets, to all human beings, and to all theoreticians
of Re-evaluation Counseling. Appreciation is due
Mary McCabe who encouraged many and inspired a
few of the poems, and to Irene, Katie and Michael,
who assisted in their publication.

--Harvey Jackins
May, 1973

PREFACES

To "The Human Side of Human Beings"

The Re-emergent Human

At peace with all the universe
Yet filled with zestful fire,
Serene with past achievements,
Alive with new desire,
Aware of distant galaxies,
A pebble I admire.

The past informs and reassures.
The future beckons bright.
I face all human misery
And plan to set it right,
The genius of humanity
A constant, fresh delight.

I know the past and plan ahead
Yet live the now that's real.
I act by thought and logic.
I just feel the way I feel.
I don't confuse these separate things
Nor wind them on one reel.

What scars remain from long ago,
What fogs still clog my brain
Yield to the daily tears and yawns
That let me think again.
My use of all my gains includes
Continual further gain.

To "The Logic of Being Completely Logical"

Cold logic? No! For logic knows to care
And care effectively. It's fear that's cold,
Illogic cringe, short-sighted, selfish, failing;

Nor is there warmth in sympathy to share.
That's just the throbbing of distresses old
In tune with ours, agreement with our wailing.

Only the zesty, eager human mind
Will always notice, care, and move to action
For self, for loved ones, and for all Mankind.
Warm logic brings success and satisfaction.

To "The Postulates of Re-evaluation Counseling"

The world today has many brilliant people
Who come to false conclusions with their brilliance.
Sometimes their logic falters where a pattern
Of old distress deflects their thinking process,
But often they can claim their logic flawless
If they omit to question their assumptions.

So it behooves us, too, to look most sharply
At what we start with when we do our thinking,
And publish broadly the exact foundations
On which our growing structure is erected.

To "The Nature of the Learning Process"

O Parents, Teachers, and all such Instructors,

Permit them learn.

                Each mind is thirsty-eager.

If never blamed, nor scolded, nor negated;
No single "No!" nor "Wrong" to leave confusion;
No disapproving frown to mar affection;
Each grows more thirsty and more eager always.

A little at one time is knowledge's portion
And that related to things known already.
No more until the last has been digested,
Related, understood, communicated
Back in the learner's words to the instructor.
Without this nothing justifies proceeding.

Once understood, new portion offered swiftly
Lest boredom's tarnish dull the mind's quicksilver.

Banish all tests, all grades, all kinds of ratings.
These only rate environment and teacher
But deeply confuse the learner about learning.

Love openly and well the eager learner
And twice as much the one whose hurts prevent him.
Loved and approved, he'll find a way to discharge.
Then let him weep and shake and laugh and temper,
And treasure the keenness of the mind emerging.

To "Guidelines"

How shall the humans of the future live?
Without distress, in love and zest and peace?
Of course they will, but mystical good-will
Is not enough. We have a lot to learn
Of practical details. We must divide
The work between us in rewarding ways,
Allow, encourage growth in everyone,
Yet know the wishful fancy from the fact
Not won to yet. No one shall be oppressed
Nor be imposed on, yet shall all contribute,
And workability shall bring accomplishment.
The techniques of community we fashion
May guide the great Community to come.

To "Is Death Necessary?"

ANTI-REQUIEM

Why

die

?

To "Co-Counseling for Married Couples"

Each to the marriage brings his hope of love.
Each hopes for warm awareness that will heal
His childhood wounds upon a tear-soaked pillow,
Embraced in understanding arms. Each seeks
And yet by now is unaware of seeking.

Each yearns, and yet compulsively refuses
What his beloved yearns for, cruel denial,
Recording of the times he was refused
When help was sought from others long ago.

So up the middle of love's blissful garden
A thorn hedge grows. Old patterns strike and tangle
And those who loved and reached are walled apart.
In every home, to some degree, a wall.

We've learned to let distresses peel away
And free ourselves, regain our humanness,
Resist conditioning and re-emerge.
We counsel well with new friends. Those we love
We find more difficult, their hurts confuse us.

With spouse there's greatest chance of most confusion,
Yet chance of greatest gain and most reward.
The thorn hedge can go down, the warmth come through.
Each can fulfill the other's hopes completely.
Respect and love each give and take, unwalled.

To "The Flexible Human in the Rigid Society"

The ways of our society
Are not all as we'd have them be.

A new society could be
A new kind of rigidity.

Only distresses made us hate
And fear and not cooperate,

And, since each human rigid grew,
Society grew rigid, too.

As we emerge from old distress
To individual happiness

There's time to think about the key
To taming our society.

To "All the Time in the World"

Sure, hurts will come, and oftener when we venture.
The crucial option lies in how we meet them.
Avoiding all the damage that we can,
We face what did occur un-numbed, unflinching,
Call loving, skilled awareness to our aid
To feel and discharge all the recent blows
Plus all the old ones that the new have rankled
And, turning insight on the gaps thus opened,
Reclaim vast areas of our lost potential.

To "Letter to a Respected Psychiatrist"

To really care
Means to dare
To share.

To "The Communication of Important Ideas"

Warm, loving humans everywhere surround us
Fogged in by fossil fears from old distress.
From out of our own dissolving fogs, turn to them,
Appreciate, approve, love, touch, caress.
Their eyes and ears will struggle to come open.
Knowing themselves again, they'll grasp our word.
With tears and trembling, stormy talk and laughter,
They'll move with us to act on what they've heard.

To "A New Kind Of Communicator"

What we have always wished were true is true.
The things we've always wished we could, we'll do.
The Universe belongs to us. We've all the time we need.
There's just confusion to dispel, some powers to be freed,
Some pain and anguish to be felt as out of us it passes,
Some knowledge to be widely spread through our
                                        co-couns'ling classes.
To the ones who guide this process our attention's here
                              referred,
Re-evaluation Teachers, key spreaders of the word.

To "Multiplied Awareness"

Alone and dull, if I but seek and find
Attentive eye and ear and open mind,
Confusion clarifies,
Awareness multiplies.
I give attention and am paid in kind.

To "Who's In Charge?"

Up from inanimate, out of one-celledness,
Gaining complexity, structure and plan,
Changing, evolving at last to intelligence,
Maturing, we make it to Woman or Man.

The struggle, repeating each fresh generation,
Exposes each one to distresses and pain.
When healing is blocked then illusions anachronate
Delude us that past situations remain.

Large, we feel little. When safe, we feel threatened.
Informed, we plead ignorance. Free, we hear chains.
Powered, we act helpless. We cling to dependency.
While ours gather dust, we trust someone else' brains.

Idiot societies bully and threaten us,
Herd us through ruts of disaster and blah,
Inflaming our scars to secure our conformity,
Blindness perpetuate, unreason raw.

Once only heroes dared rise up occasionally.
Now, all who read this know how to discharge.
Who guides your steeringwheel? Powerhouse? Universe?
If it's not you, then just WHO IS IN CHARGE?

To "The Human Situation"

Intelligence can count the neighbors' sheep,
Or bore two mountain tunnels so they meet,
Can shrewdly estimate the sun's interior,
Or measure, well enough, galactic atoms
A million parsecs distant.

                    Close at hand
We've had more trouble grasping things that matter.

We've not thought clearly about humans ever
In our recorded or suspected history.
                              Here,
Where the small group of us, by accident
Were moved to let the healing process flow,
Assisting and not hindering for a change,
Some rifts in this confusion have appeared.

These are rifts only yet. Confusion still
Persists when humans try to think of humans,
But these few insights, though beginnings only,
When checked with mirrors, periscopes, and logic
Are quite worth passing on to one another.

These glimpses can be critical to progress,
Can give one's effort purpose and direction
Much as the handlines staked for mountain travelers
Can guide to safety round the foggy steeps.

To "The Uses of Beauty and Order"

Unlittered woods, an unpolluted stream,
A fresh-swept hearth, one's body showered clean,
Soil tilled with care, tools in their proper place
Tell the real nature of our human race.

Dirt, smog, pollution, every form of mess,
These speak the presence of acquired distress.

To "The Necessity of Long Range Goals"

Afoot or horseback, rocketing or rowing,
It helps to give some thought to where we're going.

To "The Re-evaluation Counseling Community"

To think without intent to act is sterile.
To act without clear thinking prompts invective;
But while we act-think, think-act in the plural,
Ms. Carrig adds historical perspective.

To "The Distinctive Characteristics Of
Re-evaluation Counseling."

A living theory is growing, changing
As long as it is living. None should claim
To be the one expression of the truth
Since each must be conjecture.
                              Even so
A theory which states its own assumptions
And holds to logical consistency
Deserves consideration of itself
For what it really is, not through confusion
With any other system.

POEMS
OF
COUNSELING

It's Time to Win

Hey! Beloved young rebel!
Don't hurt yourself unnecessarily.
Don't spend your strength in futile blind protest
To bring on injuries and martyrdom.
You're much too valuable and dear for that.
It's time to win. A martyr's out-of-date.
Sure! There are times when risks must be incurred,
But for a thoughtful person such as you
In close relationship with other thoughtfuls
Such risk should come but seldom, far apart.
I know your bravery, you don't have to prove it,
Not once to me, nor others, not yourself.
Don't think I ever urge you stop rebelling.
That would be self-betrayal in these times
But plan to win, rely on thought, not feelings.

Fresh Look

Graceful Marie, awakening from one prison
And glimpsing of the wholeness of the whole,
Protesting cries,
                    "You do not understand!
"It all is simpler and more perfect, too,
"Than you have grasped!"

                    She reminisces on
Of sacred feeling felt the while she laughed
For days and days and days.
                    She seems to take
The feel of re-awakening for a place
She glimpsed and lost and some day may recover.

I feel amused, tho pleased, in much the way
The kids from town amused me when they came
To visit, and with great enthusiasm
Told me what fun it was to plow the field.

They walked a hundred yards behind the team
And never knew of what the job consisted
To really plow a field and do it right.

Yet they were right that plowing was a joy
And I could feel it better for their zest,
And just so now I hope that sweet Marie
In ways beyond what she has understood
May turn out to be right for all of us.

Mary's Session

"I had a fantasy the other day
Of people reaching out." She wept awhile,
"There's rhythm and there's color.
                              One could write
A play about it, or, if I could paint,
There's sunny reds, there's oranges and there's blacks.
It's almost like a dance. I used to have
Some thoughts like this before my father died.
I'd wonder when I saw a group why friends
Would not be warm and nice and reach each other.
Can't you imagine how a group could be,
Composed of every kind of human being
And all together one?" She wept again.

"I think perhaps a lot of each one's grief
Is for mankind. The whole thing's just all wrong,
The way we treat each other. Phoniness
And all these sick, sick games that adults play
Have torn at me 'til I have closed my eyes
And turned away; but now I have to look.

I guess perhaps I've always really felt
That humans mean to do the loving thing;
But when I tried to look at their unloving
It hurt so much I always shut it out
Before I understood, and it still hurts,
But now I have to cry and keep on looking."

You can.   You can. · DO IT!

You must care with your heart,
Add your mind to be smart,
Then commit the whole you to be brave.

If you're positive and loving
Your direction's pretty good,
Still unless you're really thinking
It won't work the way it should;

And although you're warm and loving
And you see the picture clear
Things won't really get to moving
'Til you contradict your fear.

You must care with your heart,
Add your mind to be smart,
Then commit the whole you to be brave.

Silver Wedding

The hands we had been dealt were stacked against us.
We never quite could see each other clear.
The models set before us to grow up by
Excelled at misery for their near and dear.

So, when I reached to love I broke your glasses
And when you spoke to help you blacked my eye,
And each one's need to grow and care and matter
Seemed wound about the other's air supply.

Yet both of us were wild to live with meaning
And neither one could stomach social wrong
And so we fought abroad as if united
And most folks thought we always got along.

All sudden now the day has come up silver,
More years together than we spent apart.
Our worst mistakes have partly been corrected.
Not quite too early old nor too late smart.

Our lovely Four are twice as tall as we were.
They think that we've done well and they should know.
They wouldn't trade us in for any others,
All glad for what we started long ago.

I've never said it well nor have you heard it,
But let me say it now and try to hear,
I STILL ADMIRE, AND LOVE YOU,
                          VETERAN TEAMMATE!
Let's try to make it for another year.

Rational Cooperation

Cooperation naturally becomes us
Until our hurt suspends our power of thought.
If then enforced, a hurt resistance freezes,
So new enforcement pressures then are brought.

Society's a harness, not a tyrant.
Men made it, blindly crowned it, wield its whips
As we regain ourselves we'll change these strictures
To happy voluntary partnerships.

Loving intelligences, re-emerging,
Appreciate, communicate, feel free,
And then cooperate the way musicians
Cooperate to play a symphony.

The Insightful Lover

To love, to really love, you have to tremble.
Only a baby's not afraid to love.
If you seemed calm I'd know that you dissemble.
It's not me nor my love you're frightened of.

All people in the world have felt rejection
When crossness from a loved one lashed our hearts.
To each new love these old hurts raise objection
For fear that hurt will follow if love starts.

So turn your back on numbness and composure.
Let tears and shivers fade the old alarms.
The wounds of love will heal within our closure.
Wide-eyed but brave, come trembling to my arms.

Ho - Ho - Hoaahum

I yawn off old primeval ooze
With yawns that pass up through my shoes
From far beneath the floor.
One fleeting glimpse of lovely slack
And then the glug comes oozing back
And I must yawn once more.

Some day this junk will all be gone
And I won't need to yawn and yawn
To keep from going blah.
Till then my constant goal must be
To cherish and approve of me
And my wide-gaping jaw.

The Future-facer

If time runs shallow,
Fleeting fast,
Why plow the fallow,
Sterile past?

Why, groping down
Worn ladder rungs,
Inhale the breath
From dead men's lungs?

Why gaze behind
At spent commotion?
Ahead lies warm,
Inviting ocean.

Don't Believe the Hopeless

There is a way to not blow up the world.

There is a way for all of us to live.

Only compulsive feelings seek disaster.

Only old scars inflame towards destruction.

Only the frightened dig the fall-out shelters.

Only the ones so full of frantic feelings,

Endured so long that all else is forgotten,

Polish the panic button, count the warheads.

Thinking - Loving

Cold logic? No, it's Selfishness that's cold,
Shortsightedness that hopes to gain for self
From other's loss or hurt or from neglect.
Not logic, but illogic this, old fears
That lose the wide world grasping for the speck.

Nor is old Sympathy so warm as sense.
It's sloppy maudlin drawing on one's old
Own hurts to match another's with pretense
Of caring but actually being introspective.

No, only human wit and mind and brain
Are true guides to the paths that are effective
Best for himself, best for those close, for all.
The rational human re-emerges strong
Steering a straight course, seeing beyond his nose,
Caring effectively to right the wrong.
Warm logic guides him everywhere he goes.

Auf Wiedersehen

Wherever you may go my love goes with you
I'll always know you as you really are
It isn't distance separates two humans
What we've attained is good both close and far.

Your judgment is superb, your eyes are open
All things will work out for you as they should
For all their lives the boys will bless your action
You're brave and smart on top of being good.

Come back and touch again in time's fulfillment,
From now 'til then I'll wait to feel that touch
And as you daily reach to love you fully
Know that I love you now at least that much.

To All My Loves

My goal is to love everyone I know
And get to know as many as I can.
Sometimes, of course, the old fears make me shrink
And wince as I anticipate reproaches
From cultural patterns.

                          Mostly, it doesn't happen
And when it does, it's only patterns thrashing.
You each know you yourselves love many loves.
You must know that I do the best I can;
And, really, I hear more approving sounds
From all of you than I used ever hope for.

So, fearfully or boldly, I shall try
To keep on loving more and different loves,
And try to feel the love you give me back.

Holding a Direction

Each one I've ever known wears despair
Somewhere about him, wrestling with it daily,
And some do private combat only, feeling
That decency forbids exposing others.
While some will hide it from the world at large
But stab and beat those closest to them with it
As if it were a clay pot they could break
From off their heads upon their loved ones' strength.

Some dramatize despair instead of living
The noises that they tried to call for help with
Have now enfolded and engulfed the human,
Insistent hopelessness, embraced and championed
Enforced, destructively, on all who near them.

Some few have raised this to a theory,
Constructed new philosophies of funk.
Their literature has futile, hopeless endings
With little sprigs of "we must still be brave",
"Though all is futile, we can still be kind"
Which sometimes brings them literary prizes
And followings among the insecure.

Yet all of this despair is vicious nonsense,
The grey discouragement which winds our ankles,
Yammers within our heads and sags our spirits
Is only ghostly shapes of childhood terrors
Only scratchy recordings of those bad times
When as dependent children we confronted
A world our store of knowledge could not cope with
When parents turned into despairing robots
And still looked like our parents, leaving us
To face a universe gone mad about us.

Holding a Direction (Continued)

These frozen memories re-echo in us
And are exchanged in daily conversation
But not to any purpose nor to good.
Traveling another route we came upon them
And viewed them from their point of origin
And saw without mistake their empty nature
And after much discussion and much discharge
And putting all our clear spaces together
We have a rule that works unfailing for us.

"Always be positive, be optimistic,
Always speak good, always encourage, praise
Always lead our and others free attention
To what is reassuring and inspiring."

To do this is to stand against confusion--
Dark, pseudo-thoughts and feelings will assail us
From out our own distresses and from others,
And if we stand insistent on the up-beat
Those burdened with despairs will come converging
From miles around and pound despair upon us
Apparently to force compliance with it
But really hoping we will stand against it
And force chinks in their gloom and loan them courage.

Ourselves need weep and yawn and storm and shudder
But, as we hold our bearing, all around us
Reality will lift and show its nature
More positive than the stand we took on courage
More reassuring than we dreamed or hoped for.

Society

Vast harness we contrived for common effort
And yoked and trained and warped ourselves to fit,
It's served, however crudely, for survival
But we have almost lost ourselves in it.

A Workshop Love

A workshop love's a very special love,
A tender growth in soil prepared with care,
All gnawing predators fenced firmly out,
Warmth, moisture, sunlight portioned to allow
Each love to flourish to capacity.

And always they do flower. Step by step
They dare to love one other, then three more,
Finding some favorite first and then discovering
That everyone's a favorite.
                              Planted out
Into the real world's cooler, drier soil
They root and thrust. They firmly spread and grow.
Green pinpoints grow to splotches on the brown
And touch and merge.
                              A parched and desert world
Recovers. Love takes back its habitat.

Tick, Tick, Buzz Tick

I used to feel a sympathetic pang
Of feeling deep within my viscera
At mangled grasshopper or trod-on worm,
Parental voice replaying in my head,
"How would you feel if it were done to you?"

It was a great relief to finally see,
A score and more years after, that the worm
And insect didn't suffer as I suffered.
Beautiful bits of wound-up clockwork creature,
Immune alike to hope and fear and pain,
I own them, brothers, still, or cousins rather,
But they don't function as we humans do.
They stopped evolving at the clockwork stage.

The mammals, though, are something else again.
They do feel pain and fear and shame and anger.
Their brains are on the edge of human function,
And though I eat my steak and roast with zest,
I don't like thinking of the death that brought them.
Someday I hope my steaks and chops will grow
In nutrient solution in a factory,
Emerging from the broth, all sliced and frozen,
No casualty more complex than a cell
No mammal's death due to my appetite.

What got me thinking this way, though, was this:
I rode the trolleys back and forth to work,
And sometimes played a game of seeking contact
With fellow riders' eyes. It isn't often
That you can get some real communication
Just in a look. They're mostly plugged back in
To their own bothers. Once or twice a week
At best I got a pleasant glance or two
That meant a human being looked at me.

Tick, Tick, Buzz Tick (Continued)

A sharp glance came more often, but its sharpness
Was often just a spinster's loneliness
Alert for forage. Other times the look
Was hopefulness a listener is at hand.
I listen all day long and while I travel
I neither want to listen nor be listened to
I only want to catch awareness out
And feel I'm not alone. The other evening
As I surveyed the usual withdrawn faces
And watched the tension patterns ripple there
I suddenly became aware that these
Moving repeating patterns that they wore
Were like the clockwork of the grasshoppers;

Not sprung from nucleic acid molecules
In insect ova but wound up to tick
In old distress experience long ago.

So when I ride the trolley now my game
Is thought of differently. I try to be
As human as I can. I look and probe,
Successful if upon the homeward ride
I coax one human for at least an instant
Outside his ticking grasshopper costume.

A LONG
TIME AGO

Peony Petal on the Tablecloth

Deep hued, the rose shades interlace
With veins of wine. As silken velvetry
To fingertips, the texture of its face.
Soft edges flow in lovely symmetry
Unflawed, unscarred, perfect in every grace,
The evening meal's dessert of poetry,
Fallen on the tablecloth beside my place.

Come Join Me on the Prairie

There will be sounds of summer winds in grain,
Brown rolling slopes, some owls and prairie dogs
Alert upon the agate-dotted plain.
You'll learn the pleasant way a cayuse jogs.

To lifted eyes the little badland buttes
Show faintly blue some fifty miles away.
You'll see the brown Big Muddy where it chutes
Through willowed **sandbars** shining green and gray.

A band of horses dots the distant swell,
A herd of cattle clusters round a well.

Orange cactus flowers throw a color splotch
Across the hard pan. There are roses, too.
We'll lie amid the buffalo grass and watch
The prairie eagles coasting down the blue.

Sonnet for Cadre Material

To you, my friend, your interest just aroused,
Greetings! From a lair of foggy thought
Woven around you year after year till housed
Almost complete, from slimy newsprint bought
To spread untruth and muddle, lift your head!
Humanity is marching, on the move,
Workers, free from confusion, in the lead.
Come take your place within the ranks and prove
Your life has purpose. We have need of you
Whether in classroom, office, factory, or hall,
Chem lab, church, or long soup-kitchen queue
You find yourself. Unwavering through it all
The struggle runs. Seek in yourself to find
A human champion, tempered to serve mankind.

The Night the Falling Drill Rig Almost Hit Me

Looming suddenly beneath his hood
Death caught my eye,
Impaled me like a mounted butterfly.

All my machinery paused in the middle of a tick
The wheels and cogs frozenly phrasing,
"How unexpected!"

The freeze went on and on
It dragged and dragged, persisted and persisted
Nausea edged the blankness.

Suddenly, Death
Lowering one soft white eyelid
Over one deep green eye
With "See you later" friendliness
Withdrew.

Exhausted, I rested apart
But all the little wheels and pumps within
Whirred and throbbed in riotous celebration.

Heat Wave At Fort Peck Dam

When it's hundred and five at midnight
And a hundred and twelve by day,
    Then the wind's quick flare
Singes skin and hair
    And dust flies up and away.
Each choking breath is a fight.

    The clerk who's awake in his bed at four
Is asleep on his desk at noon.
    The men in the pit can't soldier it,
But they'll begin passing out soon
    For the glory of government and its god,
    contractor and his profit.
    The project's one hell of a place in July.
I'll be awfully glad when I'm off it.

The Affairs of Youth

I
The gossips all whisper,
Then hush.
They look down their noses
In poses of diffidence, think naughty thoughts,
And then blush.

———————————

II

Shame on you! Shame on you!
You did what no gentleman should.
You might have been quiet if you couldn't be good.
You knew it, before it all started, was wrong.
You've told on yourself, go away, get along!
Shame, shame on you.

———————————

III
The late comer should always stand abashed
He'd heard, and so he stood abashed
Altho he didn't feel that way. He had felt guilty
When secrets still were secrets. Now that they
Had torn shirt-buttons, told it all, clean-breasted,
Guilt seemed a thing quite foreign.
                                        To have loved
Assumed a normal cast, an air of beauty.
To ever have considered taking less
Than all that had been offered would have been
Craven, almost obscene.
                                But still he made
A little gesture to old custom. He
Mumbled that he was sorry.

———————————

IV

Our kind of triangle might be described
As two large, nearly right base angles
Pried open by a slight apex intruder.
From the apex I'd like to ask one base
To give a little from his right-eousness,
Relieve attenuation, and with the third,
Mutually adored supplement of our sum,
Attempt to form an equilateral.

THE

MEANINGFUL

HOLIDAY

On Special Days

If every day could be a day of freedom,
If childhood eagerness could leap from bed
On every golden morn
                              Then every day
Could be unique, no one marked more than other.

Patterns, however, left by unhealed hurts,
Have lain upon us throughout our existence
And been restimulated by monotony,
So days merge greyly into indistinctness
Unless some action's taken.
                              Long ago
Some rebel genius came up with the notion
Of making some days special, days of rest,
Or days of worship, days of celebration,
Some days for saved-up merry-making, mourning;
And people everywhere seized the idea.

The greyness creeps back when it can, of course,
And dims the holiday with booze or commerce,
But meaning still attends the very concept
Of days especially saved for being special.

We used these times to try to say to others
What we thought needed saying.
                              Thus, these verses:

1955

In this quiet corner of our Galaxy
Where stubbornly-won gains of upward climb
Brought crystal, cell,

                Then slow-evolving creatures
Reacting each more vigorously to its world,
At last a strain that didn't just react
Emerged.

           Man, crippled from the first
By hurts begun in earliest infancy,
Persisted, and in labored social groups
Made gains the hard way.

              Two millenia back
A Teacher thought and, by example, taught
YOU WILL DO BETTER FOR YOUR OWN
    SURVIVAL
IF YOU TAKE CARE HOW ALL THE REST
    SURVIVE!
-- A golden logic, widely now revered,
Though not yet widely practiced.

                              In our times
We lift a new tool, finding that, together
We can undo each others hurts, and start
To live in zest and love and satisfaction.

The more we do the more it seems we can.

To all our partners in this enterprise
Towards Reason,

                         MERRY CHRISTMAS
                    AND GOOD CHEER
Our thanks for having known you.

                              Fresh successes
Attend you in this coming year, and fun
And no new hurts.

                         May our next holiday
See all of us giant strides along the way.

1956

This year was spent

                    One twelve-month of our time,
One free ellipsal swing around our sun,
One tiny arc turned in the Wheel's rotation.
How was it spent?

                    Did some from long-held terrors
Creep out, and trembling, walk to sureness, laugh,
And dare to live a little?

                    Did a few
Who bided in deep sorrows timelessness
Respond to warm concern with pouring tears
And, thawed, set wondrous selves once more
                                        in motion,
Knowing again that no loss loses all,
Nor lasts forever?

                    Did corrosive hates
And angers flare within the deadened walls
And burn out with no harm to anyone,
Allowing thus, ex-prisoners, in relief,
To see that what is hateful is the hurt
And not the human?

                    Did some crippling pains
Relax and mend as strained and tired bodies
Dropped tension's desperate load and turned at last
To expert healing of themselves?

                    Did those
Who undertake to walk ahead keep watch
That they not drag behind, that none alone
Can move a clear course through the maze
Of hurts, that dwindling, yet deceive us sorely?

If even a few raised clearer eyes to see
The farther, beckoning goals, put surer feet
On paths that lead to progress, surely then
The year was good.

                      Here at least we felt
The friendliness and warmth of all of you,
The unstinted help in times of crisis, too.

Here we surely saw the leaping gains
As person after person moved and moved
Away from hates and pities to the kind
Of workable concern that makes of humans
Something a thousand-fold beyond a human.

This is the time of year we celebrate
The year's end, and a birthday party too
For One who said, more clearly than the rest,
That in concern for others lies the way
To full concern for self.

                  A Happy New Year
And Merry Christmas to you, every one.

From These Beginnings--1957

On some frontiers
                    the tangled vegetation
Resists and then makes way for human dwelling
Before the swinging or the pushing blade.

On some frontiers
                    the surging rocket's flame
Lofts the experimental craft thru airy ocean
To where the sky is black at noon and midnight.
Where radiation floods, where shine, untwinkling,
The myriad brilliant stars.

                    On some frontiers
A shadow atom, limned upon a screen
Of sparkling logic, yields to patient trying
Upon itself of mathematic process,
And, bowing to the Mustness of the Is,
Offers its nature for constructive use.

Between the winter solstice and the New Year
Our custom leads us yearly to observe
A Birthday, honoring an old frontier,
One long ago begun, but little progressed.

Once was a time when stars and trees and atoms
Were present as a Man was born.

                    This Man
Spoke, forcefully and to the point, of Men,
And of the treasure yet to be discovered
In caring for the others of one's kind
As much as for oneself.

                    These later days
We have begun to pioneer the how,
And to prove Practical what has been Pious.

No one, it seems, has ever been conceived
Except serene and wise, eager and loving.

Only the hurts, the cruel accidents,
(Imposed by yet-unplanned environments
And by the older pawns of older hurts)
Obscure the buoyant happiness of living.

Never alone, but joined together, we learn
To melt and heal the aching, prisoning scars
And plan the way for future generations
To grow unscathed,

When all who live shall be
As children are beside the Christmas tree.

Some fifty billion times a child was born
Since first upon this planet Man was Man,

Some fifty billion warm and human hearts
Released to love and live, to plan and progress,
To reach with tiny fists for all Creation,
To slap the reins toward their inspired dreamings.

Yet each, emerging in a world inchoate
And in the care of those whose sweet affection
Is alternate with cruel insanities
(As scars of their old wounds inflame and torment)

Is slashed and torn at,

                     And his dear confiding
Films over with a web of anxious fear,
Of hurt, of self-doubt, of suppressed resentment.
Until each lives, a stranger and apart,
Within the steel cage of a private prison.

(This prison grows as he grows, and prevents
His ever laying grasp upon the birthright
Of love and triumph that around him beckons,
Yet whispers always with the voice of fear
That it alone, the prison cage, preserves him
From threats that still might strike because they did.)

To the undoing of this poisoned lattice
We have addressed ourselves these several years,
Learning to use the vision of another
To call the signals to the caged one
So he with tears and trembling, anger, laughter,
May free the jointed steel and, understanding,
Lift out the bars, dismantled from within.

The signal most desired nor dared to ask for,
The word least often heard and most required
Is just another's confidence unshaken
That we remain the wondrous selves we were.
That all our weird reactions and distresses
Are not ourselves but burdens that we carry.
That someone on the outside understands
And sees us with concern, not condemnation.

Each Christmastime we somehow make approach
Once more, through all the din and clamor
Of huckstered sentiment and frenzied sale,
To that calm time when wise man and when shepherd
Revered the Child, essential Human Being,
Beloved offspring of the Universe.

For a few moments only, for an hour,
Or for a day we feel again the awe
Of goodness still uncluttered,

Feel again
The lift and swell as our trapped selves respond
To what we are in essence.

You, who read,
You are beloved by all Creation, too,
You are as good as Goodness' meaning reaches,
You are secure, your fears are long ago,

And, in your latent wisdom, when another
Calls and reminds you of your destiny,
You will respond and lay your scars aside.

Christmas--1960

How strong we really are, how independent!
The World responding to us all around,
In Man's and Woman's high estate resplendent,
Informed, experienced, confident and sound!

Once, it is true, we crouched in childhood terror
Before experiences not understood.
Once, small and uninformed, we chose in error
To do the only things it seemed we could.

But now, though fossil feeling drone and whimper
That we must still be as we chose in stress,
Reality, with all its lovely interests,
Calls to enjoy the present happiness.

We are not just past crises' hurt resultant,
Though that mistake has passed for theory.
Hurt and confused, we still have grown and progressed
Enmeshed, we still have power to set us free.

Within, Man's healing process stirs and reaches,
Eager to weep and tremble, laugh and storm,
Grasping to mesh with someone else's awareness,
The re-emergent miracle perform.

Frustrate, Men reach and seek the wide Earth over,
Begin, retreat, as no one offers aid.
The others' kind concern masked by their tensions,
Their helping hands pulled back, confused, afraid.

Yet once a spark is struck of understanding,
Once the whole picture be, though dimly, seen,
Then each of us, by effort, can be helpful,
And, in our turn, by help, emerge serene.

Our project, friends, has grown and gained and
    prospered
For ten years now and still it does progress,
Built by <u>your</u> gains and by <u>your</u> contributions,
A rational island rising from distress.

When Christmas comes each year our land arouses,
Though briefly, to the caroled song of Good,
Responding to the Real through the Symbolic,
Sensing what was and will be understood.

This Holiday let's mark our clear direction,
Commit ourselves to move against our fear.
From all of us, a very loving Christmas,
To all of us, a confident New Year.

Christmas--1961

Ho! Christmas! Shall we this year be content
To celebrate your welcome interruption
Of routine tasks and moods, with drowsy beaming?
Shall we deplore the loss of childhood's wonder
At deep-piled snow and gleaming tree and tinsel?
Or shall we, more sophisticate, condemn
The busy merchants and the picture tube
For selling Christmas to us at a profit?

Could it be possible for us to pause,
Having occasion of the holiday,
Not to reshuffle our old attitudes,
But actually to notice that the Present
Is different than the Past has ever been?

That Now is New, and We are quite Unique?

Not one of us a shepherd, not a Magi
Not a medieval page-boy trudging snowdrifts,
Not a Bob Cratchit, not American children
Sleighing with jingling bells to Grandpa's farm house.

No more at bay with our environment
Lest our thin numbers and our wobbly cultures
Should be wiped out by weather or disease,
Our numbers are secure. We crowd the planet.
Can we live in the Present with each other?

Each man on Earth today, each child a-borning
Grew from one cell from which grew you and I.
Can we lift heads from backyard fallout shelters
To heed the promise of the Christmas sky?

Here where we work the picture shows most clearly
How wondrous humans are, how deeply hurt,
Each one of us a happy, loving genius,
Each one of us hemmed in by old distress.

This logically requires that the others,
Those "Others" that we fear "like automatic"
When fear-arousing slogan coats the news,
Are also wonderful, and fear-distressed.

Can we wake, interrupt our frenzied arming?
Stop playing back the threats to counter threats?
Reach for these other humans' understanding,
Avoiding the ready trap of our own fears,
Meeting their fears with our understanding?

Jesus of Nazareth lived long ago.
Our tasks are now, but we can well imagine
His words as though for our encouragement.

"Love one another," and "Unto all peoples."

Christmas--1962

The whole world talks of love but seldom acts it
They yearn but they've become afraid to try.
They sing set songs and act out ancient ritual
And fail to look each other in the eye.

The suburb speaks of "needs" with stilted accent,
The rock-and-roller beats the sad guitar,
All mumbling signals of their desperate hunger
To be accepted as they really are.

What else the meaning of the world's religions
Beneath the hurtful nonsense that they wear?
"Complete acceptance," "Love ye one another,"
"You all are cared for, for each other care."

In every cult and church the walled-off humans
Reach out. In every town and countryside,
In studio and lab and learned discussion
They seek afar the love sealed up inside.

When holidays come 'round their pulses quicken,
Their eyes unfilm a little and their fear
Backs off a bit, for Christmas is Official!
It's Right to act like friends this time of year!

And, though the parasitic profit patterns
Untune the bells and leer from Santa's eye,
The Season's tide of hope for love still rises.
They reach for meaning in the gifts they buy.

Is there a way to get to Unaloneness?
Can each one's fearful envelope be torn?
Is there a way to put the dream in practice,
The ancient dream--Humanity Reborn?

There is an island of unusual people
That's rising from the sea of wide distress,
Unusual only in the tools they carry
To help each other to unique success.

The island had some very slow beginnings
And yet persisted while its knowledge grew.
Today our numbers multiply more quickly,
We're bolder in the reaching-out we do.

Around the state and land the word is passing.
Our new friends learn much faster to be free,
And messages have come from distant countries
That people there respond the same as we.

This year has been a good one. All around us
Mankind is waking up. There was no war.
Co-counselors are smarter every session.
More folks are loving and are loving more.

Our love to all of us this Christmas season,
Our warm respect for all that all have done.
A whole lifetime of full awareness 'waits us,
A world of independence, love and fun.

Christmas List

I'd like a little bravery for Christmas,
The nerve to love my neighbor as I could,
To be friends with black and white
And not just on Christmas night,
The guts to stand for what is right and good.

I'd like a little humanness for Christmas,
An open window to my fellow men.
I'd like to dare to care,
Warmly smile instead of stare,
Have my great delight in people back again.

I'd like some fresh awarenesses for Christmas.
I'd like to taste the air and see the sky,
Smell the rain and feel the sun,
Treasure people, every one,
Make the contact live between the world and I.

I'd like a little confidence for Christmas,
Get that thrill of knowing surely all is fine,
Know things only feel that tough,
That my best is good enough,
That there's lots of future waiting down the line.

Prologue

Our leader died, a cruel and senseless death,
As festering hate and prejudice spilled over
To kill, then kill again with new excuse,
And slavering noises creaked across the land
As scars of all the past intolerance,
The vicious violence that, all our history,
Has dragged America down and held her back
From her full greatness, strained to throb again.

Yet this time, from the first, the voice of Reason
Spoke and was heard and kept on speaking clearly.
The picture-tube, that hardened blah-purveyor,
Sensation-mongered now and then but mostly
It brought the sober words of sober men
Saying we each must question first ourselves
Why these things happened, how we can prevent them.
It brought the grave new leader, squaring shoulders,
To grow into his job. It brought the crowds,
The mourning crowds that gathered in the cities.
It brought the music of memorial concerts
And pictures of the skies and fields and children.
A nation wept before its television.

Oh, our beloved Country, you have been
A long, long time in coming to your greatness,
Yet, unmistakably, you are maturing.

The year has been a thinking one for us
Here near the center of our mutual project.
Some concepts that were goals now operate
In almost daily fashion. We can say
What we're about more clearly to more people.

The human being is completely good,
No contradiction, no destructive drive
Built in at all. His special gift is just
To cope with ever changing circumstance
By endless new response, precisely crafted
To deftly master, mold, and manage all
As far as knowledge serves him. When his zest
To know and master more leads him beyond
His present knowledge, accidents occur
And do him hurt in person or in feelings.

If not destroyed, he draws back, shifting gears,
And turns to self-repair. He weeps, he trembles,
He groans, he rages, laughs and yawns and stretches,
The indications of profound untangling,
Of healing and of re-evaluation
That clear the clutter, untie tension knots,
Return his mind to function with new knowledge.

Only the hurts left unrepaired within
Adults who had the early charge of us
Emerged to frustrate each in infancy
With "don't cry," "be a big boy," "That's enough,"
And many other "do not heal" commands,
Which, lifted off by logic and by knowledge,
Allow us now, belatedly, to heal.

The human being's mind is vastly brilliant.
The human being has a joy of living.
The human being loves to love and share.

Beginning, each of us, in his own tangle,
Our progress was, at first, by indirection;
But, as our knowledge and our gains accrued,
We steered more straightly and for longer reaches.
This year, some corners turned may be the last.

To underline again familiar knowledge,
The hurt recording never is the human.
From first to last, for counseling to work
We can't regard the Person as a Pattern,
We can't regard the Pattern as a Person;
And this must so remain and still hold true
For the first person singular, the self.

To love, to really love, to pierce Aloneness
With child, with lover, or with group affection
Pushes us out from every hurt recording,
Chronic or not. If this resource be there,
The clear direction is--love and be loved.

An even sturdier road has opened wide.
All patterns reek of self-invalidation.
So, to appreciate ourselves defies them.
Still more, to set one's mind to hold
By previous commitment to express
In words, tone, face, and posture our complete
Appreciation, with no reservation
Of our own wondrous selves secures our compass.
Alone, with friend, or with a counselor,
The same direction holds, all patterns shatter,
Discharge abounds. We act as if we were
Already free.

                    Ahead the thicket thins,
The light shines through.

As you love us.   We surely love you all

          A Zestful Christmas to you!

Christmas --1964

Now who will claim the leadership of men?
Which leaders will we follow as we strive
To shed the tangles and the blocks and blindfolds
That cumbered us before our strength was grown!

Will we surge happily to fall behind
The one who calls to easy lack of thought,
Who pats and beams upon our prejudice
And bids us yearn the past, who meets a plea
For justice for the poor and aged and dark
With wit that always wowed the locker room?
Apparently we won't.

                        Within our nation
We seem to have decided to keep growing,
To risk exploring if new thoughts might help
To meet new problems.

                        This alone would make
The past year notable, but there was more.
Some gains in civil rights, a bill was passed.
The endless murders done in Mississippi
This year were publicized, though not prevented.
No world-wide war exploded. This gave time
For more growth of the slowly firming notion
That there need be no wars at all.

                        Abroad,
New nations started and old nations grew
More independent. All the vicious fabric
Of white oppressing dark showed still more threadbare.
Only a few new nations still invaded,
New slogans, new excuses pasted over.

The poker club of those who bid with atoms
Enlarged itself unbidden. It begins
To look as if some contact might replace
Our lack of contact with eight hundred million.

Who will be leaders of the wide earth's people?

The ones who say and mean and prove in practice
That every single person in existence,
Of every stature, hue, and inclination,
Shall have the best of treatment from us all,
That there shall be no difference shown except
For help to overcome the past mistreatment.
These are the ones the earth will take as leaders,
And they'll deserve that leadership in full.

You, dear beloved, who hold equal power
With every other human on the planet,
You, whose warm confidence and loving wisdom
Is eagerly awaited by the rest,
How helped you cage injustice this last twelve-month?
What leverage-points found you to right old wronging?

II

A rational island rises from an ocean
Of old confusion passed on by contagion.
A group of people, rising, lift each other
To dreamed-of heights of loving, thinking, acting,
With hands outstretched for others still to join them.

Here on the island growth accelerated.
The firm directions we uncovered last year
Have held up very well. In every instance
That one tried to express appreciation
Of his own self, and kept on so attempting,
In happy tone, good posture, pleased expression,
Distress discharged both then and in between times,
And progress and improvement were consistent.

New groups took root spontaneously and functioned.
A lot of goals from past years were completed
And higher, new ones set.

                    New friends have joined us.
Our first book seeks a publisher at last,
And four new pamphlets are in circulation.

The island people who are moving fastest
Have learned to love more boldly and more deeply
And love more people in their daily practice.
The ones who hesitate and wait and waver
And come back later, we now realize
Will hear and move, too, when the theory reaches.
So we must plan to say things still more clearly,
Apply more that we know to what we're doing.
Then all those near can come on board together.

You, special one, whose being and direction
Alone are quite sufficient for insuring
The end of all unreason if the others
Were not already with your undertaking;
You, center of concentric universes,
Who mans the master console of our project,
How boldly did you stride since last stock-taking?

How far flashed your example as a beacon?
How many came ashore and joined your sector?

It's Christmas time once more, and we're reminded
Yet once again that Mankind's slow emergence
Is sought and hoped for, not by just a handful,
But by all people--each good, eager person
That waits behind each mask the wide world over.

Form and Content

If my Christmas is to have some meaning for me,
If my Christmas joy be more than empty smile,
Can I turn to Tree and Star and ignore the wrongs
                                        there are
While I beam at ancient symbols all the while?

Can I fondly smile at mine and neighbor's children
And forget those in the central part of town
Where restrictions and despair hang upon the
                                        ghetto air
For the children who have faces black or brown?

If my "Peace on Earth" be more than thoughtless
                                        mumble
While I work one day in ten to pay for war,
Can I possibly agree any man's my enemy
Or that any goal at all's worth killing for?

If the Christ Child were to come this year in person
To my church and home and to my working crew,
Would he feel that he'd been heard, or might he
                                        leave this word-
"You sing my Name, please live my meaning, too"?

Year's End--1965

This year the century's big change continued.
By tens, by millions, humans made decisions
To stand no more for treatment as inferiors
And in their various ways and various countries
They made their moves to live what they'd decided.

The fears of those who feel a stake in stasis
Cried chaos, leaped to label, pleaded neatness,
Called for delay and, where retaining power,
Used cattle prods, police dogs, bombs and napalm,
And sent young men to die in unjust battle.

Oh, mourn we must for every fallen fighter,
Marine, guerilla, Mississippi martyr.
No one should die on an oppressive mission.
No one should have to die for peace and progress.
Still like a tide, resistless, Freedom surges.

At home, new legislation cleared old road-blocks.
Health-care when old, concern to halt pollution,
Support for art, a better start for children,
Attempts to keep the poor from getting poorer
Are now official programs for the future.

Here at our job, a year of better answers.
The workability of the great project
For freeing every human from Unreason,
For claiming, using every great potential
Was always evident, showed on each person.

The Pilot Plant for People, still enlarging,
Drew many more to join and moved all forward.
New pamphlets have been added. Some are teaching
Who hardly yesteryear could dare be students.
The first book is in widening circulation.

Three useful insights are our gifts this Christmas,
Of greatest use to those who've come the farthest
But meaningful to everyone who grasps them:

The first,
              Each person at each moment bygone
Has always done the very best he could do,
(If one allows for the whole situation)
And so deserves no blame and no reproaching
In any way.
              The second,

                        Looking forward,
We always have a choice. The future, forking,
Permits us freedom to choose fresh and wisely,
Knowing to act by logic, not by feeling,
By discharge we escape the old compulsions.

The third,
              Our own good judgment, working always,
Can be consulted still in any upset.
Remembering theory and resisting feelings,
We can consult ourselves and ask the best way
A genius such as we could choose to function
This very moment.

                        Have a Merry Christmas,
A New Year full of love and life and progress.

At Two-Thirds of the

Twentieth Century

The hastening flicker of our nights and days,
The social rock twixt Progress and Reaction
Tends to obscure the spiraling advance
Of humans, of Society, and of the Cosmos
With trivia and feelings of distress.

So at stock-taking time we surely probe
Beneath the platitudes and public snow-jobs
To not call evil good, nor call war just,
Make clear the wrong directions and the dangers
No matter how we're pressured to applaud them;

And just as surely we probe deeper still
Beneath our worries and discouragements
About the wrongs that keep on being wrought,
Permission of our fears and in our names,
To sound Reality, to basic process
That moves against the hateful present crimes
As new-born mountain, rising from the sea,
Carries the marks of waves to alpine heights.

First, are the young men going out to kill
And die in Asia for the cause of Freedom?
Of course they're not! Conditioned fears and slogans
And blundering strategies are but the trappings
Of too-quick profits. War's great wastefulness
Is crutch and cane to sick economy.
Too many poor at home, so vast investments
Are made around the world, then backed by guns.

Until some braver politician shouts,
Loudly enough to pierce the slogan-din,
Some peaceful way for even bigger profits
War's lumbering disaster lacks a brake.

The profits trickle widely here at home.
We keep our welfare check or Cadillac
And mute our conscience. Not Victoria's British,
Who smugly watched her armies gut the world,
Nor Hitler's Germans sharing loot from Europe
Were more complacent than the Gallup Poll
Reports Americans are. Step up the war!

Yet this is surface.
                    Struggling for expression,
America yearns for peace and hates wrong-doing.
America wants her sons home safe, un-calloused.
America wants the right for other nations
To organize themselves the way they wish to
Whether it pleases us at all or not.
America hates the role of cop-and-robber.
So when last month America had elections
America cast a vote against the war.
The air is blue with counter-explanations
But every thinking person knows it happened.

In all the world this war has no supporters
Except the satellites and bribed dependents.
So, though appearances seem all despairing,
Great forces move for peace, and peace will come.

The drive for freedom of American blacks
Is also pictured to us as defeated,
And we are told white prejudice has backlashed
And that white liberals are alienated
By black men's haste and militant demands.
It's true that ugly prejudice is showing
In towns whose names seem novel in the headlines,
But prejudice had long been operating
And only snarls when challenged and uncovered.

83

It's true that many pledges of performance
To finally apply the Constitution
To non-white citizens as well as white ones
Are put aside or broken or forgotten.
It's true that nearly all the great pretensions
To root out sapping Poverty's infection
And stop the spreading blight that spoils our cities
Have been abandoned for the Asian madness.

Yet no real progress has been lost at all.
Exposed pretensions and destroyed illusions
Confront us only with reality,
For Negro suppliance and white sympathizing
Were never on the road to anywhere.

So sharpening black voices will keep sharpening,
And confidence and dignity and strength
Will rise behind them. When the white decision
Is made at last for fairness it will come
From sheer enlightenment and plain self-interest.

This year saw more attention to pollution.
Some thrilling steps to space were taken this year.
Few people starved, no world-wide epidemics,
And several million humans learned to read.

Our pilot plant for humanness recovery
Ran fuller schedule this year. Our alumni
Stormed many heights, accomplished great
achievements.
Some, half a world away, held firm direction
And found groups formed around them by contagion.

We know of many children who are growing
Almost without distress. Group work advances.
Classes are largest ever, learn more quickly.

We speak more widely and are heard much better.
A second printing of the book was ordered,
The how-to-do-it book is being written,
And, every moment of the day and evening,
Someone is counseling or being counseled.

The Isle of Reason lifts, extends, and prospers.

Reality supports our cheerfulness
For all is well and on its tortuous journey
To being better.
                    On these holidays

Our love to all and thanks for love accepted.
A happier Christmas and awarer New Year!

An ancient call, the watchman's reassurance,
We call to you this season -- ALL IS WELL!

And all is well each moment and each season.
Reality is real. It simply is.

The past was as it had to be. Complete
The way it was, it calls for no regretting.

Nor is our future pre-determined ever
But, rather, forking endlessly before us,
Invites us to take charge of what will happen
By fresh anticipations and wise choices.

(It's true that hurt recordings press upon us
To pin us still in rueful, useless struggle
To wish the past undone or dim the future
With narrow vision hemmed by old distresses;
But we can free each other from such traces
With expert ease by now and claim our freedom.)

NOTHING UNSOLVABLE AHEAD

The matrix which evolved us still supports us.
Our lovely planet, scene of life's emergence,
Sweeps on in orbit stable to our nurture.

We humans now are billions and old habits
Will not suffice for present nor for future,
Yet simple thoughtfulness and simple changes
Transform what's hurtful to our benefitting.
Polluting wastes can turn to soil enrichment,
Trash, junk, and scrap convert to raw materials.

Environmental cycles, undisrupted,
Will keep our great space-vessel fresh and lovely.
The fusing atom's vast and useful power
Is only months away from being harnessed,
Sufficient energy for every purpose.

The pyramid of life, our fellow species,
Need not extinguish from our hungry crowding,
But, rather, flourish with wise conservation.
Our food chains can be simpler, shorter, harmless.
Illuminated sheets of flowing algae
Can feed great vats of yeast, a daily harvest
To underwrite the milk and eggs for billions
And leave room for all living things to prosper.

VANQUISH THE ULTIMATE FEAR

Does fear of death depress you? Those who perished
Were wondrous fortunate to ever have lived.
To be alive's a boon, however fleeting.
Sometime, and soon enough, some small adjustments
Will be worked out within our body functions
And we'll have immortality in practice,
Fulfillment of man's ancient expectation
Not in the glittering fantasies of heaven
But in perpetual health on earth,
                                    For dying
Has never served a useful role for humans
Since we could think. Death's not a good escape hatch
From old distress when we can lose distresses
Helping each other weep, and laugh, and tremble.

HASTEN THE END OF WAR

The peoples of the world are turned to freedom
And soldiers in our name stand in their pathway
With guns and planes, with ships and tanks and rockets,
Most grievously in far away Viet-Nam.
A hundred lies exhort support for slaughter,
But lies grow tired and thin and people sicken
As napalm rains its fire on helpless children.
So patriotic arrogance is wilted
And those twin push buttons called Fear of Others
And Fear of Change are worn and function feebly.
More brave young men choose prison than be drafted
And politicians talk de-escalation.
This war will halt and soon all wars will end.

COMMON CAUSE COMING

Black liberation movements won't be halted.
The current nationalism serves its purpose
Of forming an identity and program.

When formed and firmed, then unity will come
As white and black make common revolution
To change society to serve all people,
Learning in common cause to love each other.

THE ROAD TO REASON

World-wide we humans stir towards re-emergence
From old irrationalities to Reason.
A thousand movements start and reach and falter.

The one that's called "P.C." by those who know it
Is special in that here the means are tackled.
Solutions aren't just talked about and wished for
But found and used and taught and passed to others.
That crucial knowledge which each new-born infant
Knows well, that tears must flow and fears be
                                         trembled
And angers stormed and laughter well and sparkle
Before the hurts can go, this precious knowledge
Is shared and taught and put to use consistent.

We've much enjoyed new friends who joined us this year.
The groups where all give each the help to discharge
Now span this continent and occur on others.
Some able, influential new arrivals
Have widened our horizons, raised our prospects.

We seek new quarters now to ease the crowding,
Designed to serve our functions more precisely.

New publications are in preparation
To make first contact with our future fellows.

AND A RATIONAL NEW YEAR

You who have taken part in these adventures,
Persist, for greater treasure lies before us.
Set ruthless schedule for your own emergence
Apply your tools with vigor and consistence,
And make and keep warm contacts with those others
Who have not grasped as yet the means for freedom.
Communicating will complete your knowledge.

We love you all and cherish your affection,
And all of us together love all people
Not just with sentiment but thoughtful action
To put our love effectively in practice.

This Christmas is a time for love and sharing.
This New Year is for goals and reassurance.

Much love, much cheer, much reassurance to you,
A year of brighter goals and deep fulfillment.

Holiday Communication -- 1968

the basic, positive premise

    Our human goodness is beyond destruction.
    It shows in many ways in every person.
    Only the scars of unhealed hurts conceal it
    And, though the scarred behavior can distract us,
    Beneath it, pulsing, struggling, seeking freedom,
    Fine minds, warm hearts, a zestful joy of living
    Persist and seize each chance to melt the shackles.

we live in a dying, outworn society

    The crumbling social systems that surround us
    Make fierce pretense of strength the while they
      stagger
    Like children's tops that reel before collapsing,
    Exploiting, killing, wasting, and polluting,
    Enforcing individuals to their madness.

    Yet though with force and shame and pious urging
    They strive to herd us to resist the future,
    Demanding in the names of Gods and Customs
    Accompliced crimes against ourselves and others,
    They only fool us by mis-information.
    We only serve them where distresses dull us.

look what lies before us

    How precious is the goal of human freedom!
    How overdue the end of exploitation!
    How close at hand the end of all mis-treatment!

the end of all oppression of man by man

Not one child ever bruised or shamed or scolded,
Or hungered, lonelied, thwarted, or neglected.
Not one skin hue esteemed as less than lovely.
All proud for each for being male or female,
And every person's culture and experience
A contribution to the common treasure.

Pride in a nation cast aside like crutches
In regained health and pride in being human.

our environment, no longer abused, will be sufficient for all

Our world becomes a lovely spaceship garden
Tended with thoughtful care and satisfaction;
Wild areas left in plenty as insurance
That nature's processes shall function freely,
Each living species treasured as a brother,
Each resource that we tap improved by tapping,
Each used material cycled back for re-use.

freedom of the individual from distress patterns

To play our role in Liberation's triumph
Requires of each a personal liberation.
The patterns of distress and thoughtless action
We wear from our old hurts must be
    dispensed with.

not "easy"

It's never easy to cry out our sorrows.
The courage, time, and counselor's attention
Are hard to put together and persist with.

Our fears are fearful and deceptive to us.
To feel and shake till unafraid's not easy.

Our angers and embarrassments and tensions
Resist and cling and burrow back within us.

but always workable when truly attempted

> Yet always does the process work profoundly,
> Each barrier yielding to persistent discharge,
> And the great gains of hundreds who've persisted
> Lend confidence in starting to the timid.

all are welcome to the fellowship of re-emerging
humanness

> Welcome! to you who have been looking for us.
> Welcome again! to you who hesitated.
> Much love to all of you, our close companions.
> Our fellowship projects the Future's people.

an account of the pilot project usually called "p. c. "

> The year was good. We've never been so busy.
> Home base expanded and new outposts started.
> Groups have a place to meet and more assistance.
> Classes were large and varied. Our surroundings
> Have neatened, brightened, beautified around us.
>
> Some sharp companions joined the staff to help us,
> While others, far away, began new centers.
>
> The world-wide drive for human re-emergence
> Continued finding clear expression with us.

greetings for christmas, 1968 and new years, 1969

> In love and satisfaction and achievement
> We greet you at this Christmas celebration.
> May next year bring an end to all the killing,
> May racism die out from Love and Reason.
> May each of us achieve a full year's progress.

Holiday Greetings -- 1969

To everyone: Sweet words of confidence!
Mankind survives and will survive and flourish.

The dissolution and decay around us,
Pollution, bigotry, and war's destruction
Are symptoms of an outworn social structure
In process now of crumbling and replacement.

Even the individual who most repulses
Beneath th' enforcing shroud of old distresses
Is kind and good and thoughtful, lovely, loving.
He simply waits the skillful touch to free him.

Only effects of being hurt, mistreated
Make humans into problems. Stop mistreatment
And problems will be stopped. We need to love,
To love with thoughtfulness, with skilled persistence.

The humanness called counseling expanded
This year to new dimensions. Classes flourish
With brave new teachers growing to the challenge,
In new locations, too. A wider audience
Listens and reads and questions. Groups are growing.
Co-counseling is a part of life for thousands.

The deeper questions of our human quest
Involve a score more thinkers than in past years.
Never an obstacle appears before us
But yields if we apply our knowledge to it.

Be bold! Be confident! Use love and judgment.
You are in charge of these, your universes,
And we are all together.

                              Merry Christmas!

End 1970:

Right on to Next Year's Promise

No stopping now.   The time of preparation
Has ended its first phase.   We turn a corner.
The long years gone when we were just a handful
Living on resolution and persistence
And on the counseling we gave each other.
Few listened to us then or dared to try us
And often these tried out of desperation.

The word wings wide now, workshops multiplying.
The mails move literature in all directions.
More elementary classes than we know of.
The oceans spanned to London, Honolulu.
Psychiatrists, psychologists are with us.
Now patients group in hospitals to discharge
And college students take exciting courses,
Co-counseling for academic credit.

Respected scholars speak at world conventions
While men in prison pair to laugh and shiver.

We face new tasks to handle new conditions.

One urgent need: to put more present knowledge
In writing, published, and in circulation.

New forms of contact and communication
Must be devised to keep close touch with thousands
As yesterday we did with scores and dozens.

As theory spreads wide it risks dilution
By well-intentioned, unaware insertion
Of pattern or confusion by the teacher,
And we must find some loving ways to check this,
To keep our clocks and compasses together.

And in the midst of all this new excitement
We must take care to care, to love each other,
To love ourselves, to see to rest and leisure,
To melting of our own remaining glaciers.

We have long thoughts to think and time to
                                        think them.

Much awkwardness is past.
                          A path is blazed
High up our mountain's side. The lower slopes
Are thronging now with swiftly mounting friends
Who need not risk a single precipice
Nor wander in confusing thicket long.
The loose rock slides we bruised ourselves upon
While slipping, floundering, and re-climbing still
Are roped and posted.
                          Knowledge is abroad.
Printed and published, passed from hand to hand
And, though this knowledge grows and will keep
                                      growing,
We're past the crucial period of discovery.
The drudging years of find-out-how rewarded.

The second kind of climb has been concurrent
For many of these years--the outward-reaching,
The passing-of-the-word, the hand-extending
To bring our friends and kin on board the project--

And this, though crucial to our own progression,
Was not so easily perceived as such;
And shyness, lack of confidence, and self-
                              absorption
Delayed and slowed our outreach for a period.
But wet wood dries at last and fires grow hotter
And in these later years the word spreads swiftly.
Not only do we realize the need for outreach
But learn to forego arguing and urging
In favor of the magnet of example
And of the sample session freely given.

The third stage came before we realized it.
Co-counselors are more than individuals.
Recovery bares the need for loving contact.
Community arises willy-nilly;
But our communities are for the future
And little of the structures that surround us
Is useful to us.
                          Currently we ponder
Each new step in the rational construction
Of frameworks to support and spread our caring,
To speed our re-emergence and reach others.

Communities we have grow large and larger
And new ones start each week across the nation
With leaps to Canada, Tasmania, England,
To France, to Guatemala, and some others.

We give a friend a session and receive one.
The basic one-to-one communication.

In Fundamentals Class relearn to discharge,
And, when we discharge and assist our clients
To discharge well in nearly every session,

We learn to find and hold our own directions
In everything we do, the chronic pattern
Defied, confronted, contradicted, challenged.

Then, when we grasp the universe is ours
And each one is in charge, with no excuse
For any irresponsibility,
We join in permanent community
A growing, thoughtful, able all-for-all.

A fourth stage lies ahead and is beginning
The permeation of society.
Green shoots abound to indicate its coming
The church, the office, factory, prison, school
Begin to send out human-sounding signals
As humans in them join to act like humans,
Inspired by the example and assistance
Of one of our co-counselors outreaching.

A fifth stage is conjectured, when bad structures
Are happily collapsed by those within them.
No longer patient victims of oppression.

Some crises faced us this past year.
                                    We met them.
The future seems **remarkably** inviting.

Year's End -- 1972

Intelligence, that transcendental function,
Just now begins to take charge of the cosmos.
Its roots in caring, flowering in awareness,
Scanning the world with zestful expectation,
It grasps to know, experience, learn, endeavor
To create and assist creative process.

We bearers of the function on this planet
Are awkward yet about its use, forgetful
That we possess it often, often relapsing
To thoughtless primitive or hurt behavior.

No blame attaches to us for misfunction.
Hurts were imposed upon us young and helpless.
Yet, also, to emerge is purely our job,
Mutual assistance all there is for resource,
To wait for helpful god or parent futile.

A dozen thousand of us so far join our effort,
Beginnings on four continents and some islands,
Our numbers doubling faster than expected,
Much cause for satisfaction, none for stupor.

New problems rise on old solutions' nurture.
Fresh thinking's daily needed in our project.
Each battlefront we open 'gainst Unreason
Opens us to confusion's infiltration.

Clear thinking for a group means policy.
Policy starts with individual thinking,
But needs discussion leading to agreement,
Sturdy commitment, flexible application.

Events nor patterns need not dictate to us,
Policy-armed, our keen minds operating
We'll sift the People from the Patterns deftly,
And take charge of events and of the future.

More To Come

New thoughts to think, to celebrate,
To ponder, change, communicate,
Will keep emerging each new year,
And I shall want to make things clear.
(By the urge to be heard I was early bitten.)

Poems will continue to be written.

GLOOM
AND
DOOM

Frustrated

Continually, continually I find myself in trouble.
There is no sense nor recompense
In using such true instruments
To try to please those malcontents
Who see their visions double.

If I were young, naive and good
And held my tongue as told I should
A lucky guy were I,
But well away and lack-a-day
The devil's out and hell's to pay
Impelled to question why.

Regretfully, regretfully I let the matter pass.
There's no reward but no excuse
And droning patterns' dull abuse
Re-knots the fetters I would loose.
I trudge through the morass.

Sunk in the Chronic

It really doesn't matter that the years
Have fled so swiftly while I wandered, dim.
It doesn't matter that my griefs and fears
Crippled me unaware. My hopes are slim
That anything about me ever mattered
Or ever yet can matter. All my fret
And busy-busy frantic use of time
Has only been distraction I regret.
My brother was beloved, the family's head,
And when he died our family warmth went out.
My mother wished that I had died instead,
And since that day I've always stood without
And wished that I, too, had a right to live.
Ashamed always of having failed to die,
I seek excuse by what I try to give,
Needing anew each breath to justify.

DOGGEREL

Jingle For Thinking Social

A rigid Old Society
Is not the way for you and me.

A human doesn't need a whip
He needs a happy partnership.

To My New Windsor Loves

I love you, everyone of you,
Love every mother's son of you,
And every father's daughter, too.
You'd be amazed how much I do.

I love to look into your eyes
To catch your first thoughts by surprise
And pull them out into the air
While laughter cascades everywhere.

I love patrician Beth Soley
And Frances (Sex) Bartholomay
I love the Moulton's, Joyce and John,
Their willingness to be leaned on.
I love Lynn Sherwood's supple grace
And Liz's open, loving face.
The eight-foot octopus named Devine
Will always be a love of mine.
Above the group he looms alone.
Think what he'll be when he's full-grown.

My yen for Wells cannot be hid,
Both Stephanie Still- and Mary Sid-.
Fresh dreams arise with little risk
As fantasies of Dreama Frisk.

I love responsibility
When someone wears it besides me,
And where the usual limit quits
Why, that's the place where Richard Fitts,
And Barbara Fitts another place,
Epitome of charm and grace.

From her real self she'll not turn back,
Beloved, clear-eyed Jo Kilpack.
I toast the Yost I love the most,
But which? Why, back and forth I coast.
My love for Smiths I will not curb,
Smart Jean, brave Doug, and super Herb.

While Kris brings terrors out to light
I like to hold her hand real tight.
With sisters Snipes I cannot lose
We all love all, no need to choose.
Esme will lay it on the line
When it is demonstration time.

Marilyn, Rebecca, and Suzanne,
I'll be with them each time I can.
Beautiful Inge of the lovely song
Just lets things happen as they come along.
I've loved her longest, and love her strong.

John, behind proper speech and stare,
Is cuddly as a Teddy bear.
While Brinton, Lu is small, perhap,
But feels just right upon my lap.

Betty's warmth unfurls, uncurls,
We both love George of the gorgeous curls,
Even though he distracts my girls.

Lovely Carol, brainy beauty.
I don't love her from a sense of duty,
And my affections most enlarge
To level-headed, caring, steadfast Marge.

And surrounded by all this wealth
I'm even drawn to love myself.

Instant Historical Perspective

We humans have been muddling on
A million years or less
Not yet knowing where we're going
'Cause we started in a mess.
While our brain case was expanding
And intelligence developed
We kept getting hurt and frightened
So our brain with fog enveloped.
We've acted awfully stupid.
And still do so today
But if you doubt our progress
Just look back along the way.
For millenia we were cannibals
And for millenia more
We kept sacrificing humans
To appease our gods with gore
Then we bought some leisure, knowledge
For a ruling, priestly few
With the slavery of the many
(And some places we still do.)
Later slaves emerged to serfdom.
Then the serfs threw off their chains.
We began to talk of freedom
And free use of human brains,
But still children worked in coal mines
And in textile's dusty mills.
Exploitation and oppression
Spawned continued social ills.
Still our struggles have persisted
Until in our favored land
Or at least for favored people
There are some things that are grand.

Only three-fourths of earth's peoples
Still must worry about food
Or must fight for freedom from the creeps
Who rule "for their own good".
Racism blights its victims
And its perpetrators, too,
But its victims are rebelling
And will have support from you.
Only less than half our people
Do not have enough to live,
And a lot of children go to school
And pass on through the sieve.
Still, there's slack enough in places
To at last begin to look
At what goes wrong with our thinking,
Why we took the route we took.

February Mountain

Once fourteen people climbed a sunny mountain
And lived a week above a spreading ocean
And looked into each other's eyes and wept
And shook and stormed and laughed and touched and loved.

Tall, bearded Carter made the longest journey
His gentle wit and smiling courtesy,
His keen intelligence and quiet correctness
Lent strength to all he touched, gained as he grew.

While Polly with her loud voice cymbals crashing
Moulted the boyish shell to find the woman
Voiced shrewish feelings for her own amazement
Suffered withdrawal pangs, took charge of loving.

And Mary, three years old and innocent
Gazed wide-eyed at the world, did as expected
But finally shared the old and ugly feelings
Left by antique reproach, began to thaw.

Bill played the role of clown when pattern had him
But keen eyes peered and peeked through his disguises
And gentle strength and quiet persistence gave
The lie to raucous laughter: Bill stood tall.

Jean Andrews came a lady, left a lady.
Her discharge came and went with dignity--
No wild abandon yet for her, more thought
Comes first. Jean knew what she was doing.

While Nikki drove and swam, buzzed in and out
Turned cartwheels in the road and changed her mind
Assured in every move. A humming bird
Moves round a vine or hawk with equal grace.

Attractive Sherri, frozen in pretense
From old rejections, felt her fingers pried
To leave the shell, face new reality.
Sherri! Come out and join us, let us love you!

Tall viking Harvey, looking thirty years
Reached for the precious feeling of all-rightness
Beneath the crummy little feelings plaguing
From ancient scoldings all his seventeen summers.

And good scout Barbara, far from usual comforts
Lived puritan and spartan, shed her sorrows,
Blazed with occasional righteous indignation
And then wept lest her blaze had hurt her loved ones.

Tall Robert, equal parts of brain and panic
Caught now for years in rationalized postponement
Accepted leadership, endorsed the now,
Began to straighten shoulders for charge-taking.

Soft Sheila translates everything to hugs,
Some hugs a paragraph and some a sentence,
Her lovely self emerging from the lonelies,
Her confidence recovering in the sun.

Pat didn't cook a meal. She washed no dishes,
For one week didn't drown in tending others,
And all the gains of discharge and emergence
Were only frosting on that blissful cake.

While Gloria B. , shy bird of paradise,
Tackled a dozen fronts, denying always
That she had any problems she could work on
Except to see that Harvey was protected.

Benita couldn't join us. She'll come later.
Some visitors spiced up our stew, Scribe Roger
And Gloria Z. , and Marilyn and Lucy.
Each gave their own refreshing contribution.

While elder Harvey, sniffling, soaked the sunshine,
Enjoyed the smallest workshop known, napped often
And volley-balled and 4-squared to contentment,
And fell in love with thirteen lovely people.

SONG LYRICS

Father-Daughter Banquet
(sung with Sarah to the tune of "Muss 'i Denn,?")

Oh father, oh father,your daughter has grown,
                      daughter has grown,
No longer a child is she.
From baby to toddler, from tomboy to teen,
                      tomboy to teen,
She's become a young lady.
To college or altar soon she must go.
She cannot with the family stay.
Look deep in her eyes and tell her your love,
                      tell her your love,
Before she's gone away.

Oh daughter, oh daughter,your father is shy,
                      father is shy.
He's not sure that you still care;
And misunderstandings too often arise,
                      often arise.
You've been in each other's hair.
So reach him before the years can conspire
To wall him away from you.
Look deep in his eyes and tell him your love,
                      tell him your love,
Before this evening's through.

Dear people, dear people,the walls must go down,
                      walls must go down,
That keep us all apart.
Hurt feelings and shynesses must not conceal,
                      must not conceal,
The love that we felt from the start.
Appreciate, validate, cherish, approve.
Take time for some hugs every day.
Look into each other's eyes and speak of your love,
                      speak of your love,
And close to each other stay.

Light-hearted Lyric
(to its own tune)

In the spring! Oh, in the spring!
When the bees and bugs and birds are on the wing,
Then his heart begins to glow and in his chest it
                                    burns.
In the spring a young man's fancy lightly turns!

When the snow begins to go
And the leaves and grass and buds begin to grow,
Then the young male of most any species yearns.
In the spring a young man's fancy lightly turns!

To thoughts of art, of politics and fun.
So many things to think about, why concentrate on
                                    one?
If there's green grass below and blue sky above,
He may accidentally, coincidentally, sometimes think
                                    of love!

There are wars and threats of force
From imperialists the whole wide world abhors,
But though a youth his duty seldom spurns;
In the spring a young man's fancy lightly turns!

The Lonely Prairie Windmill and the Moon

He was a lonely, creaking prairie windmill,
And she the mistress of the evening sky.
There in his place he drudged at common labor,
While she, in cloudy robes, went sailing by.

He yearned to know this radiant silver princess,
And stretched his vanes toward her in the night,
But scorning his harsh shadow and his dullness,
She hid behind a cloud her lustrous light.

'Til once her cousin Sun
Laid waste the prairie land
With curse of summer drought.
From all around
Earth's thirsty creatures pressed
To the giant who knew no rest
As he drew life-giving water from the ground.

The moon looked down and saw and learned to
                                        love him.
So now he creaks to her a happy tune;
And their love affair goes on, every night from
                                        dusk to dawn,
The lonely prairie windmill and the moon.

117

Complete Appreciation Song
(To the tune of "The House I Live In")

I am a human being.
It's the nicest thing to be.
The world went on evolving,
And at last came up with me.
I'm smart, I'm brave, I'm thoughtful,
As loving as can be.
A lot of people love me,
And it's just because I'm me.

The beauty all around me
Is there for me to share.
The life between the grass roots,
And that cloudy vault up there,
The paintings and the music,
The books and poetry
Are all for my enjoyment,
And it's just because I'm me.

I'm a happy human being.
I'm sure I'm here to stay.
I kept on working, trying,
Got some breaks upon the way.
Now I'm re-emerging
To a life that's good and free.
You know that I deserve it,
And it's just because I'm me.

It's fun to be a human.
It's fun to be alive.
It's nice to find the exit
From that old recorded jive.
Though I didn't always know it,
It was always good to be,
And I'm glad that I persisted
'Til I know that I am me.

I'm living in a nation
That's very proud and strong,
Where there should be peace and plenty,
Yet where all our lives go wrong.
I know I've found the reason,
And the way to set us free;
And you'll follow my example
And be you, like I am me.

Northwest Love Song
(to its own tune)

Verse

Pleasant hours bring happy thoughts
When the blue sky is gleaming above,
And a song is the voice of the heart's intent,
So here is a song to my love:

Chorus

My darling is found
By the lovely Sound
Where the pines and mountains meet the sea.

The wind as it sings
From the mountain springs
All its fragrance brings to Dorothy.

Each of her eyes holds a star's affection,
And she walks with a fawn's perfection.
Where she smiles gleams the sun's reflection,
Tranquilly.

Her love is so kind
That I'll never find
One who'll please my mind like Dorothy.

Cry a Lot
(To the tune of ''Camelot'')

We've changed some ancient attitudes around here.
Emotion is encouraged more than not.
You'll notice if you listen to the sounds here
We cry a lot.

Brave men lose no esteem when they weep sadly.
Unhappy women loudly mourn their lot,
And warm arms hold the child who's feeling badly.
We cry a lot.

We cry a lot, shake a lot,
And we allow our children to.
We laugh a lot, yawn a lot.
We all think better when we do.

There's no put-down for crying out your sorrows.
We've found that folks feel better when they do.
In short, we've all been taught
We need to cry a lot,
And afterwards our happiness comes through.
We--cry--a--lot.

Things Are Different

I went walking down a city street.
Saw people stand on each other's feet,
Buying and selling, push and shove,
Too damn greedy to think about love.

Doodle Dee Doo Doo
Dum De Dum Dum
Things are different where I come from.

We wake up loving at first sunshine.
We do other things if we ever have time.

Went to a super-store looking for food.
Such pretty packages must be good.
Additives, preservatives, chemicals, dyes
Fill your stomach with a bunch of lies.

Doodle Dee Doo Doo
Dum De Dum Dum
Things are different where I come from.

If you farm with the soil and the sun and rain
You'll nourish your body and feed your brain.

People go 'round tied up in knots,
Using recordings instead of thoughts,
Passing on the put-downs, feeling alone,
Hurting inside with a face of stone.

Doodle Dee Doo Doo
Dum De Dum Dum
Things are different where I come from.

We know how to hug and we know how to cry.
One discharges while the other stands by.

In a little while I'll have to go
Back to that mixed-up world, I know.
They'll ask me what I'm so damned happy about
And I think I'll give them a great big shout
            and sing

Doodle Dee Doo Doo
Dum De Dum Dum
Things are different where I come from.

Something's got started and it won't stop
'Til the whole blamed world's one big workshop.

Remind Yourself Song
(to the tune of Muss 'i Denn)

Listen well, listen well to all your clients tell,
All your clients tell,
Warm attention to everything they say.
Don't advise, don't comment,
Even with the best intent, with the best intent,
What you say will get in their way.
If you listen to them well,
Then the discharge will come,
And they'll think for themselves all the way.
Don't advise, don't comment,
Even with the best intent,
With the best intent,
What you say will get in their way.

When their voices break or shake,
That's the phrase you have them take,
Phrase you have them take,
They need help for the tears to begin;
But when discharge has begun,
Quietly wait 'til it is done, wait 'til it is done,
Then repeat their phrase and say "again."
When laughter, or trembling, or tears are at hand,
They need your little push to begin;
But when discharge has begun,
Quietly wait 'til it is done, wait 'til it is done,
Then repeat their phrase and say "again."

To persist, to persist, that's the way you assist,
The way you assist.
That is one thing they cannot do alone.
When their story is through, you request it anew,
Request it anew,
Even though they're sure that they are done.
It takes a hundred recountings
With discharge to clean up each one.
When their story is through, you request it anew,
Request it anew,
Even though they're sure that they are done.

Your reward, your reward is not long deferred,
Not long deferred,
A lovely human mind set free.
Intelligence clear of sorrow and fear,
Of sorrow and fear,
Is a mighty pleasant sight to see;
And best of all you get your turn
To have warm attention, you see,
And when discharge is through to again be really you,
Again be really you,
And live the way life ought to be.

Do We Have To Act So Mean?
(to its own tune)

A group of neighbor children
Came with him to the door,
And the boy went to his father
As he'd often done before.
He said, "Dad, can I talk to you?
We don't like what we've seen.
Oh, Daddy! Just because we're white
Do we have to act so mean?"

"Since the Johnson family tried to buy
That house across the block
We kids have all been listening
To a lot of funny talk.
The Johnsons all seemed nice to us.
They were friendly, neat and clean.
Oh, Daddy! Just because we're white
Do we have to act so mean?"

"The Johnson boys played ball with us.
At first we found them strange
Because their skins were darker,
But their playing made that change.
They're fun to play with and they're good.
We'd like them on our team.
Oh, Daddy! Just because we're white
Do we have to act so mean?"

"Chuck said you had a meeting
At his house the other night,
And there were people telling you
That, just because you're white,
You shouldn't let the Johnsons in,
But build a color screen.
Oh, Daddy! Just because we're white,
Do we have to act so mean?"

"Chuck said that Mr. Bugjuice
Was the one who led the fight
And told you all what you must do,
While most of you kept quiet.
We kids know Bugjuice beats his wife,
And his yard is never clean,
But, just because some folks are sick,
Do we have to act so mean?"

"I heard the City Council was
Afraid to vote things right
For fear that, next election,
Campaign money would be tight,
But, Dad, you're braver far than that
And you don't have to run.
I've voted you in permanent
As model to your son."

"The Johnson kids said that they hope
That they can live nearby.
It's crowded where they're living
And the rents are awful high.
They say kids get discouraged
In that mid-Seattle scene.
Oh, Daddy! Just because we're white,
Do we have to act so mean?"

I'd like to say the father
Paid attention to his son
And talked to all his neighbors
'Til the housing law was won,
But, until we've faced the issues
And our City's face is clean,
The question's still--"Because we're white
Do we have to act so mean?"

We all love Belafonte
And we cheer for Davis' bat.
The first to fall at Bunker Hill
Was a man whose skin was black.
It's time for us to face our fears
And act like a human bein',
And show that, just because we're white,
We don't have to act so mean.

UNCLASSIFIED

Rock Hunt

When we arrived at Agate Beach that night
The wind was blowing fresh and stiff inshore
And surf was pounding on the beach and rocks
A million tons at once. When it drew back
Along the beach the gravel rolled down hill
Behind it 'til the next wave slammed it back,
Rock-tumbler for the world, with gems for all.

The sky and wind and weeds and sea were fresh,
And I felt just as fresh and cold and clean.
The surf seemed dangerous 'til I learned its rules
And learned that it would keep them honestly,
Then we played tag. I dared and looked for stones
Between the waves and, usually, I won.
The surf played pretty well, though, too.
                                    It tagged me
One time in four or five and in a while
Its dripping handmarks reached above my knees.